Praise for Todd Davis

. . . it's time to recognize what an important voice in American poetry we have in Todd Davis. —*Image*

As readers encounter the ordinary miracles that Davis reveals as both father and son within "the kingdom of the ditch," they also are reminded that the human is not apart from nature but a part of it. —*Chicago Tribune*

Davis is unflinchingly candid and enduringly compassionate. —*Harvard Review*

Through meditations on the flora and fauna of his Pennsylvania home, Davis brings readers into a world rife with danger and darkness as well as quietude and splendor . . . He reverently observes nature's own poetry and how it illuminates the process of change. —*Publishers Weekly*

Wisdom, more than anything, characterizes his poems. —*Arts & Letters*

Like poets Wendell Berry and Mary Oliver, Davis is committed and spiritually anchored to his home ground, and so the language rises organically from his daily life. —*Orion*

These poems are really lyric meditations on the way life and the world turns, done in stillness yet shared through a poet's trust in the world and the word. . . . We can only be grateful for this music of living, for such a song and such a singer. —*New York Journal of Books*

Davis hunts, fishes, and observes nature in the great tradition of Robert Frost, James Dickey, and Jim Harrison, among others. His poems lead us from the tangible to the intangible and about halfway back again. —*Gray's Sporting Journal*

Gratitude and wonder radiate from each of Todd Davis' poems, rendering them sacraments for readers lucky and open-hearted enough to receive them. —*basalt*

NATIVE
SPECIES

Books by Todd Davis

POETRY

Native Species

Winterkill

In the Kingdom of the Ditch

Household of Water, Moon, and Snow (limited edition chapbook)

The Least of These

Some Heaven

Ripe

ANTHOLOGIES

Fast Break to Line Break: Poets on the Art of Basketball

Making Poems: Forty Poems with Commentary by the Poets,
    co-edited with Erin Murphy

SCHOLARLY

*Kurt Vonnegut's Crusade, or, How a Postmodern Harlequin Preached
    a New Kind of Humanism*

*Postmodern Humanism in Contemporary Literature and Culture:
    Reconciling the Void*, with Kenneth Womack

Reading the Beatles: Cultural Studies, Literary Criticism, and the Fab Four,
    co-edited with Kenneth Womack

The Critical Response to John Irving, co-edited with Kenneth Womack

Formalist Criticism and Reader-Response Theory, with Kenneth Womack

Mapping the Ethical Turn: A Reader in Ethics, Culture, and Literary Theory,
    co-edited with Kenneth Womack

NATIVE
SPECIES

POEMS BY TODD DAVIS

MICHIGAN STATE UNIVERSITY PRESS ▪ *East Lansing*

⊗ The paper used in this publication meets the minimum requirements
of ANSI/NISO z39.48-1992 (R 1997) (Permanence of Paper).

Michigan State University Press
East Lansing, Michigan 48823-5245

Printed and bound in the United States of America.

28 27 26 25 24 23 22 21 20 19   1 2 3 4 5 6 7 8 9 10

LIBRARY OF CONGRESS CATALOGING-IN-PUBLICATION DATA
Names: Davis, Todd F., 1965– author.
Title: Native species : poems / by Todd Davis.
Description: East Lansing : Michigan State University Press, 2019.
Identifiers: LCCN 2018020124 | ISBN 9781611863154 (pbk. : alk. paper)
| ISBN 9781609175948 (pdf) | ISBN 9781628953602 (epub)
| ISBN 9781628963618 (kindle)
Classification: LCC PS3604.A977 A6 2018 | DDC 811/.6—dc23
LC record available at https://lccn.loc.gov/2018020124

Book design by Charlie Sharp, Sharp Des!gns, East Lansing, MI
Cover design by Erin Kirk New
Cover image is *Deer Drinking* (1892), watercolor by Winslow Homer.
Courtesy of Yale University Art Gallery.

g green
press
INITIATIVE Michigan State University Press is a member of the Green Press
Initiative and is committed to developing and encouraging
ecologically responsible publishing practices. For more information about the
Green Press Initiative and the use of recycled paper in book publishing, please
visit *www.greenpressinitiative.org*.

Visit Michigan State University Press at *www.msupress.org*

For Shelly, Noah, & Nathan
—always

What I believe is,
all animals have one soul.

WILLIAM STAFFORD

Contents

NATIVE
SPECIES

Geomorphology

What does a landscape dream of in its unsettled dreams?
Of snowpack still ten feet deep. Of going to sleep
to the sound of sea-drenched wind and waking
to rain in the basement. Of yet another dream
in which nearly every room in the house
is rearranged. Boulder in bathroom. Old growth
hemlock blocking the stairwell. Kitchen faucet
turned to torrent. Caddis uncased and floating
in yesterday's soup. Fish seeking shelter
in the bedroom closet. The front porch
somewhere at the bottom of the reservoir.
And the lock on the dam picked clean.
The entire mountain sliding
into a new zip code.

I.

Almanac of Faithful Negotiations

> *Here, at the edge of heaven,*
> *I inhabit my absence.*
> —TU FU

On the first day, we find evidence of elk but not the elk themselves.

On the second, we see the charred and blackened sleeves fire leaves but not a single flame.

By the third day, the oldest trees have already ascended but the microbial mouths buried in the dirt remain.

After four days, our minds flood with rivers and creeks, and we find it hard to speak, except in mud and stone.

On the fifth, ravens decorate a white-oak snag, croaking in the voices of our drunk uncles, reminding us whose house we live in.

Six days gone, a fisher stands on hind legs, stares across the meadow's expanse, dares us to approach the porcupine-corpse, muzzle red with the body's sugar.

When the last day comes, only minutes before dawn, susurration of wind, stars moving back into the invisible, all of us wondering when we will join them.

Goat's Milk

The bells up and down the ridges
wander through the small window
in the kitchen wall. The girl who makes soap
and fudge from goat's milk to sell to tourists
who come for the fall foliage is trying to describe
for her mother, who is deaf, what it sounds like
when she slides her fingers along the slick udder
and milk spurts from the goat's nipple.
She makes no mention of the goat kid
they found mostly eaten in the rocks, how she
took the bell from around its neck and washed
the blood from the shiny metal with the hose
at the side of the house. Her father and brother
want to kill the coyote that did this, and part of her
wants that, too. She forms words with her hands,
gestures to her mother, and says with silent lips
the word *red*, because milk sounds alive to her,
and next the words *water* and *stone*, because the stream
running from the woods and into their pasture
resembles the clattering of hooves. The last word
she mouths, wrists turning over the expression
like needles knitting wool, is *risk*, the swish-
swish of milk circling the bottom of the pail,
a single goat neglected by her brother
who brought the herd from the far meadow,
the parting of grass as a paw pads
the soft turf, and the bleat from the back
of a goat's throat, moaning first out of hunger,
then out of fear.

Perception

If my life's a mere blink of the eye,
what's there to contemplate in yours?
—MEI YAO-CH'EN

A gray fox falls through river ice and drowns,

    stiff corpse floating to an eddy where the unreliable

ice that took the fox's life forms around its head

    and body. Only ears prick the slab,

which holds the shape of former suffering,

    and we look down in disbelief, our own feet unsure

of what bears them up.

Passerine

In the early sexual tingling
that May brings, a nuthatch climbs
down the trunk of a chestnut oak,
headfirst, recognizing the earth below
for its true worth. The trilling
of a hermit thrush spirals a song
through a sky of budded branches,
and my wife's hair trails across my cheek.
The Talmud teaches: "Every blade
of grass has its angel that bends over it
and whispers: *Grow, grow*." How often
do we consider the arrangement
of a bird's toes: three pointing forward
and one back? My feet are useless
for holding still, and I can't sleep
sitting up, although my grandmother did
while she nursed her sons, one born
after the other, a line of succession
without a throne. Most of us would die
if we had to roost in the canopy
or close our eyes and inch out
along the main beam
of a well-trimmed tree
shading a residential street.
Yet tufted titmice and pine siskins
slumber while clinging to the slenderest
perches or balancing on the edge
of a metal post. At this hour
it's all call and response, and soon
the moon will rise like a salmon's eye
in the white foam of clouds. A marsh
wren swims in dusk's pink waves,

lands on a cattail and bobs its throat
in a question. We've stolen
most of paradise with our opposable
thumbs. Somewhere among the tamaracks
a mockingbird mimics our endless lust
by pilfering its neighbors' songs.

Hard Winter

In January, the same day we got 20 inches of new snow,
Charlie's son Jake died, only 56 but with failing kidneys
and a bad liver that had been marinating in booze
most of his life. Charlie ended up at the hospital, too,
77 and a heart flickering like lights in a storm.
His wife baked snicker doodles for the nurses, worked
crossword puzzles and drank coffee with Splenda
while he rested between tests. Before Charlie was released,
Family Services took the Miller kids away from their uncle
who'd cared for them since their folks died in the accident
on Kettle Road. One of the divers who found the bodies
still buckled in their seats keeps dreaming he's sliding
down the mountain, going over the rail and through the ice
to the bottom of the reservoir. The uncle beat the boy, touched
the girl where he shouldn't. His hearing's in three weeks,
and the weather feels like a restraining order. Our cousin
Jimmy had four fingers go missing: third-shift drowsiness
and a machine as mean as any pit bull, refusing to let go
of his left hand until the screams told someone
to shut down the line. We got our two deer during rifle season,
but turkey will be slow on account of this late March snow
and the fact that Jimmy, the best caller in the family,
doesn't feel like slogging into the woods anymore. Sitting
on a stool at Al's Tavern, Mike, who works for Family Services,
told everybody that the Miller boy should've stuck up
for his sister because he knew how to use a shotgun.
The game commission reports it was cold enough to kill
deer ticks, ash borer, and wooly adelgid. My wife thinks
we're under attack, the planet spinning back to a time
when humans weren't necessary. Her mother suffers
from Lyme's disease, the ash tree in our front yard
is mostly dead, and the grove of hemlock near the pond

is a skeleton deer avoid. Charlie will pull through—
his father lived to be 98, his mother 92—and the snow
will melt, trout fishing good a little later because the river
will stay colder. Most things will recover. Jimmy will learn
to use a mouth call instead of a turkey box. Trees will scar over
where limbs broke off in an ice storm in February.
The rail guard's already been replaced, and the bruises
that covered the boy's body have disappeared like ink stains.
I worry about the girl, though, what was done to her
and the way people talk, a mix of sympathy and gossip, salt
and cinders thrown out by plow trucks, grass not growing
near the road, some of it torn up and needing to be reseeded.

The Woman Who Cuts My Hair

asks if anyone in my family works the railroad.
Her dad did and now her husband and son.
The engine shops employ less than half the men
they used to, and even fewer travel the trains
between Altoona and Pittsburgh. She barbers
in the family room of their house. Customers
can see the kitchen from the chair. She dries
wishbones on windowsills, and whenever someone
asks what she's wishing for, she says not to come back
as a chicken and laughs. Her husband's an engineer,
her son rides as a brakeman. Hair falls to the brown
linoleum floor, and where it cracks a broom
is useless. Every time she passes, the smell of cigarettes
floats from her blouse, and when she speaks
it's like a leather shoe walking on cinders.
She says the morning the train shuddered to a stop
her husband kept shouting *What the fuck!*
She uses a number three clipper along the back
of my scalp and lets me know she doesn't approve
of that kind of talk. But that's what he said
when he saw the man stumbling onto the tracks, wishing
it was a bear or deer, some other drunken animal
come out of the woods. She says it's always too late
once you see them. Last year a train trying to brake
derailed near the ALTO tower. A lot of people live
along these tracks. She says her husband and son
shouldn't have looked. The man was cut clean in half,
like the baby in that bible verse. With a razor
she evens my neckline, then splashes talc
to soothe the burn.

Cracks

A pickup slips over the ice, rear tires spinning, turning
a circle, then another, a series of donuts in a mechanical dance
that causes the three boys to swear and laugh, spilling beer
onto their laps and the seats that already stink of cigarettes
and sweat. Their dads and uncles sit in hastily erected shacks,
hovels spread across the lake, humped over like dirt
at the entrance to gopher dens. They fish in the half-light
of heaters, drinking schnapps and whiskey, readying themselves
for the rod to bow, hovering over an augured hole
as if it were a nest in need of guarding. When at last
the line jerks down into the dream of a northern pike,
they fumble with the reel, hearts racing ahead of an ending
they imagine will be told at the bar on a Saturday in June,
glasses of beer sweating, hands spread wide in a lie
to suggest the size of the fish whose head sprang
from the slush-filled abyss, only to escape their grip
into the black depths of late December. Air snakes
through the truck's cab, windows rolled down
so these bored boys can scream at the stars
salted across the sky. Most of the men have gone to eat
supper, to watch the Lions lose one more game on TV.
The smell of propane lingers, stirred with the beer
the boys burp as they smoke cigars and cough.
They've parked the truck at Ralph's shanty,
and the older brother spits into a plastic jug, snuff
stuffed under his lower lip, as he tells stories
about a buck he killed in October and a girl he dated
from the next town over with a mouth as soft as velvet.
There are always cracks in the ice, but trying to decide
which seam is harmless and which leads to the bottom
is a matter of luck. They've grown accustomed to the lake's
groaning, having heard its teeth chatter since they were children.

13

Sun melting into the horizon, everything refreezing
in a slick swatch of darkness. Toward the south end
of the lake, springs thin the ice, but the boys believe
the cold insures their passage. On the way back
a wheel breaks through, frontend dipping, the entire truck
tipping, then plunging forward like a duck, tail feathers
pointed at the moon. Every year some drown,
and even more trucks sink. But tonight,
with the windows open, each boy places a foot
on the seat and leaps to safety, rolling onto their sides,
praying the ice-shelf will hold. The sound of the truck
being sucked beneath the surface is smothered
by their happy hollering. None of them thinking
about the cost when Szymanski's Towing
sends a diver down with a cable and hook,
or how their moms will cry as their dads berate
such stupidity, which of course is inherited.
For now they can only hoot at their own good fortune.
Cold stars warmer with their escape, sparkling
like the fake diamonds they give to girlfriends
on six-month anniversaries. The moon offering
just enough light to help them to shore
and to the county road they'll walk
all the way back to town.

How Our Names Turn into Light

One man hammers stone

      in the middle of a quarry; another

cuts blocks from its side. In faraway cities

      monuments are constructed, and the abandoned

pit fills with water and fish. Grain by grain

      the mountains diminish. In one sacred story

Christ bends to write in the sand; today, in this place,

      clouds shadow goldenrod fringe: bees and flies

moan with the pleasures of pollen

      smeared on abdomens. With legs heavy

from treasure, it's difficult to remember

      that farther north polar bears starve

as sea-ice recedes. Where we've fractured

      the earth's scapula, grief shudders involuntarily

like an aspen leaf. Some would have us believe

      death is consensual. We should practice

gratefulness, as Basho did, who gave thanks

for teeth to chew his evening meal of dried salmon.

The wind erases most of what's written

in the sand. The rain washes the rest.

Hexagonal

Chambers laid out in wax

    like the exposed architecture

of heaven, and like heaven the sun

    shines eternally in the ambered

sweetness of what they produce.

    A sticky mathematics of sustenance.

Labor made light by the fragrance

    of a fallow field. The names we've given

to clover and goldenrod a mistranslation

    that collapses. Entire colonies

destroyed by carelessness, and bees

    flying toward an eternity

which we imagine is finer

    than a bank of purple aster.

First Thoughts about God after Spying
a Speckled Trout Eat a Green Drake

A cloud floats in a pool that turns like a slow clock,
helping these insects slide from birthing shucks.

*

Duns roil the surface, twitch and flutter,
a new born or paralytic who believes
he can rise and walk again, if only the wind
would command him.

*

Halos drift around red and blue spots
that star the sides of trout, flares
in rushing water like tongues
of flame.

*

Heron loves the river cast in green, erratic light
broken over the sycamore's body
that translates these watery scriptures
into parables of branch-shadow.

*

A fish wrings its tail, flings itself
toward the molting sky, mouth open
to a psalm of snared flies.

*

More than half the world is covered by water,
yet most of us are afraid of drowning.

For Ron Rash

Talus Slope

Even the stones speak in this field of scarlet

      huckleberry leaves. Tomorrow's *Dia de los Muertos*,

and I should be baking bread for my dead father

      whose ashes help these bushes grow. We're always eating

a portion of those we loved—leaf-stem or rabbit-haunch,

      deer that browse everything their necks can reach.

In Mexico they cook to guide the dead back to their homes.

      The last time this ridge was clear-cut

my grandfather hadn't been born. Timber rattlers take up

      dens where scree shifts in piles. In these miniature

caverns that hold out winter, ropes of snake bodies

      coil around one another, and the dawn-light

shines like the blue of my father's feet

      two days before he died.

Geodes

Loose stone slides out from beneath boots as we seek
to hold back our weight from the bottom of the ravine.

After a month of no rain, the streambeds are dry,
and the shuffling dust rises around our legs,

like the blush my mother used to prime her cheeks
before going out with my father on Saturday nights.

350 million years ago all of this was covered in water,
a tidal flat where nodules formed under the seafloor.

My mother still wears the sparkling brooch my father gave her
half a century ago. When he was still alive, he loved to trace

the path of water, to search its course for the dull, round rocks
whose rinds might hide something beautiful at their core.

Each month, before we visit, my mother polishes her wedding ring,
the glittering refraction of cut stone. She still flushes at the thought

of his body when she tells me how they made love in the woods
on their honeymoon. Often after a hike in the hills, my father

would take a geode he packed out, place it on a wooden slab
and strike it with a hammer, splitting it in two. On lonely afternoons

his death still shatters my mother, and she calls to cry on the phone.
After today's walk she takes one of his geodes from the shelf,

insists I take it home. On the front seat the sun enters
the grinning mouth of crystals and shines so bright

I have to close my eyes.

My Mother's Cooking

Most of the time we settled for Salisbury steak
TV dinners, store-bought because she forgot
to turn on the oven or buy eggs, or because
when we lifted the lid on the flour bin, we found
ants crawling through white drifts, the dishes
never done the same day, the sink filling up.
And when she did get to the store and remembered
to buy hamburger for Sloppy Joe's, blood and tomato
would spill over the mixing bowl's lip, pinking
the counter; sugar sprinkled down the sideboard's
face as she decorated cookies, gritty like sand
beneath our feet, and roaches scurrying under the refrigerator
when we flipped on the lights. There was the lard
she used to fry cornmeal-covered chicken thighs,
the kitchen smoky and splattered, grease shining
the wooden cabinets. What was left from any meal
was thrown together into a Pyrex dish
and christened *goulash*, borrowing the word
from our Hungarian neighbor who helped clean up
some of our family messes. My mother used
the entire clock's circle and then stole more hours
from the next day, staying up to read Harlequin romances
until three or four in the morning, collapsing on the couch
where I would find her dreaming of a lover,
mouth open and snoring, surprised by my kiss,
insisting that she would make toast
before the school bus came, smear peanut butter
on its burnt surface, the jar put back in the cupboard,
her brown fingerprints on display.

Failed Argument against Sorrow

Everything flows toward structure,
last ache in the ache for God.
—CHARLES WRIGHT

A year of bad news: nephew diagnosed
as schizophrenic; cousin's son dead
from a drug overdose; a friend hiking in Montana
sits down to rest only to have his heart stop.
This side of the mountain recovers its own.
Where the logging road curls, tulip poplar
and moosewood take over. Just below the center
of my chest is a hollow place. Brook trout are surfacing
in the stream-fed pond. One jumps clean out
to eat a yellow sally. It seems the aching never ends.
A kingfisher circles the water, lands on a snag
and scolds me. A red-eyed vireo plays a tune
on the piccolo stuck in its throat. So much
is hidden by green leaves, and grief
smells like creek water on skin.

Finding a Skull

A jawbone bleached by winter fails to say
what its owner thought, as death crowded
the space behind the ear. Instinct's benevolence

continues to bless: blood flows south, then north.
Hunger leads to desire. For a moment we are both
inside and outside of the body. We struggle

to comprehend the contracting population
of golden-winged warblers, but understand
the moist exhalation of an opened mouth,

teeth formed perfectly to rend scalp from bone.
How can we judge the animal who takes pleasure
in the sumptuous licking of flesh, even the eyeholes

cleaned of their meat. The new mantra of sustainability
sounds like flies buzzing on the lips of bureaucrats
who forget death consumes everything.

Loss of habitat is mostly to blame,
but hybridization with blue-winged warblers
accounts for some of our grief.

Imagine how the body opened under the nail's
razor claw, the way it scalpeled the membrane,
heart unruly and hemorrhaging. Without leaves

this early sun blanches skin, makes evident
the clear-cut's scar on the ridge.
By April the opossum's pouch squirms

with sleepy pups, and in June we'll count
warbler calls and blush if we spot the bird,
its plumage reminding us of our nakedness.

Because This Is What Love Comes To

I brush away snow to watch the pulse of water
beneath ice. We're allowed to name the stars

more than once. Look at the naked sky in January.
The light we're blind to at midday travels toward us,

broken by a cone on an alder branch, only to become
shadow. My heart sits impatiently in the basket

of my ribs, reminding me that not long ago
the pierced dark showed ships at sea

a way home.

In the Seventh Month My Mother Worries

whether I will be lost, too, her heart
heated, banging against the trellis
of her chest like the pie tins she ties
to stakes in the garden to frighten
crows and deer, the soft, nibbling mouths
of rabbits that eat each green shoot,
and though she didn't mean for it
to happen, she thinks she somehow
betrayed my brother and sister, expelled
them to small graves at the back of the family
plot to listen to the harsh whispering
of the wind in the yew tree's branches.
She'd hoped for children to grow
older with, muddy feet to walk
the rows, small hands pulling weeds,
arms filled with baskets of potatoes
and carrots, the rutabagas and beets
carted to the cellar, the thick stalks
of broccoli that remind her of the ash
trees where grackles roost, calling to one
another in a voice like her own mother's,
asking for something other than the bitter
taste of kale melted in broth made of
creek water and chicken bones. In the shadows
of her lungs, I hold my breath, crouch
behind her spleen, willing my heart
to be still, telling it to beat quietly,
while she begs me to stay, imploring
me to nudge her rib, to turn over
in my sleep so she knows I want to be
with her, so she can be assured

my brother and sister will not come
in the night to take my hand, to drag me
beneath newly turned earth, ready
for planting.

Decadence

If the ancients deny heaven treasures wine, and say
moon has never understood wine—I know it's nonsense.
—YANG WAN-LI

A fawn, no older than four days, wobbles
     to stand beneath her mother's belly, bumps
her still-forming head against the udder,
     which starts the flow of milk. The delicious
sweetness of dame's rocket, pink and purpled,
     fills the air and makes me think this is what the fat
in doe's milk tastes like as it seeps
     from her nipples into the slurping mouth
of her young. The month of May possesses
     a viscous fertility: the same fawn will run
in a matter of weeks, wine pouring from heaven
     as sun and rain. In the riffles, brown trout
stuff themselves on sulphur and coffin flies.
     While we fish we watch the water's surface—
jaws parting, bodies porpoising, a thousand dimples
     and swirls that mimic the expanding galaxy.
In the sandy banks above the river, fox and mink
     dig for turtle eggs, yellow yolk dripping from chins,
their mates lapping the evidence to sate desire.
     My love and I sleep naked in the returned warmth,
hands draped over the round flesh of a long marriage,
     over the pleasure we take in each other's aging bodies.
Two nights ago a bear destroyed a friend's beehives,
     broke the boxes and left the drawers strewn
like half-read books. In the face of this wreckage
     he laughed, told me to think of the rapture
in a pink tongue swathed in honey, of the black-armed
     stickiness, the splendid apiary confusion: bees flying

everywhere, stinging the bear's immense head
    as he reared up and grinned, licking and grinding
the waxy comb between his teeth and gums.

Denomination

Then find a name for it. Take your pick: it could be a name
from science, or one of countless folk names, or you can make
up your own. This changes everything, yourself included.
—CAROL KAESUK YOON

This neglected stream our ancestors named was named by others
who came before them, those who lived in this place

for thousands of years, whose mouths formed a language
we might have learned if our words hadn't drowned them.

Long before our image marked the water's surface, the stream
uttered its own name, comprised of sounds that trouble tongues,

an alphabet of falling water shaped by rocks and boulders,
by dead trees, rotted and washed in clean shallow graves,

by refuse collected in spring floods, by the arguments of snow
melting, the confrontation of everything converging, disappearing

toward a sea. Like us, the raven and deer, the small speckled
trout that swim in agreement with the ever-changing current,

the heron who fishes alone and the porcupine shunned by all
but its own, each calls this moving thing by a different name,

which surely translates as *blessing.*

For Robin Wall Kimmerer

17-Year Locust

When at last they split
their papery coffins,
do they call out for the sun
they've never seen?

Or are their cries a lament
for the darkness
abandoned in the husks
they cannot retrieve?

Hibernation

Snow crusts over after a day's thaw: white lines left on the sky by a
departing plane. After lunch the wind warms, despite the new ice
that covers the pond. We follow tracks that lead to a hemlock where
a pile of porcupine scat rises like a child's pyramid. With all the still
life paintings, why not the compacted symmetry of sawdust shaped
by intestine? What will we hang on our walls now that those in charge
have forbidden certain words, the names for flowers or the way the land
tilts? When we wake, we should ask what walks while we sleep. The
bear we saw in the orchard has wedged its body under a rock-slip, slit
in the snow to breathe. Slow thoughts make their way upward, sluggish,
clawing the corpse of winter.

II.

Lost Country of Light

But I am not trying to get to heaven.
I am trying to get to earth.
—CHRISTOPHER CAMUTO

June sun, so longed for in December,
paints a burning light upon my neck
as I hoe the garden or pick raspberries
along the ditches. By early afternoon
I've had enough and retreat to the trees,
into broken shadows dim as the back
of the closet where I put things
that shouldn't be forgotten: the field
where my grandfather planted beans;
the last cow my family ever owned;
the hay rake that turned the cut grass
into windrows; the bell on the back porch
my grandmother rang when she heard
her son had died in the war.

Green Beans

Two women lay on the grass with a saucepan between them.
Clean hands to strip the stems, a knife to slice the beans.
After a hard week of rain, they picked the better part
of the morning, everything growing so fast that another day
and the beans won't be worth eating. In the kitchen
the water's started to boil. Jars washed of what they held
last summer. The younger of the two thinks about Johnny.
Like his dead brother, drafted and shipped away to the Pacific.
He still writes a letter once a month, signs it with *love* and
draws a picture of an anchor. They were swimming Pikes Falls
a year ago, sharing a cigarette she hoped her mother wouldn't smell.
She asks her friend to hug her, to place her hands at the small
of her back. Not the same as his, knotted and calloused,
but she's glad to imagine him as her friend strokes her hair,
caresses the skin along the lobe of her ear.

Dead Letter to Elizabeth Bishop

You wrote the mist
was *like rotting snow-*
ice sucked away
almost to spirit,

and you were right,
all this white
thawed and frozen,
thawed and snowed on,
and today drifting up
in melting fog.

We haven't seen
bare earth
for five months,
and the river
only opens
where the springs
melt ice.

We fish these holes,
eat enough
to keep body knit.

The soul slips
its fingers
from the wool
of winter, unshucks
and floats above
the sleeping frames
of flesh, the idle
smell of sex.

In the slowing
streams of blood
a woman dreams
of a daughter
and full cupboards,

a man of a boy
who might help
with fences
and spring
planting.

The Alzheimer's Patient Tries
to Remember the Names for Trees

On this late April afternoon, when the girl
she thought was her daughter, but was actually
a neighbor paid to watch her, left the porch
to use the bathroom, the woman lifted herself
from the rocker, shuffled down the narrow stairs,
away from the house and into the woods.
Beyond the spit of grass she called for her mother,
as she'd done when she was lost as a child.
The deeper she trailed into the forest she traced
grooves on the bark, fingers stroking boles
where they flattened and flaked. Somewhere behind her
voices shouted her name, but she ignored them
and followed the path of the sun. This first warm day
the earliest leaves unfurled, and since she couldn't
recall even the commonest tree—mountain-ash or sassafras,
sourwood or witch-hazel—she began to rename them.
Chestnut oak became *scallop tree*; a small hawthorn
was dubbed *needle-bush*; and serviceberry, with its slender
white blossoms, the *doily tree*. It was beneath these branches
that they found her. Hands moving back and forth
in her lap, as if she held a crocheting hook. A smile
on her face as she worked on a baby's bonnet
for the child she told them was expected in June.

What Came Before

My Cousin Speaks in Dreams

The warmth of a blood-filled sky.
A westerly wind. Half-moon, smooth
as melon rind, floating above
father's head. A boatyard
with a sea beyond. My sister,
who worked for a shipwright,
lathering varnish onto a keel.
A pod of dolphins surfacing
beyond the harbor's mouth.
And a fig tree with ripe figs falling,
seeds mashed beneath
grandmother's bare feet,
her way of planting
a memory that would leaf
in my tenth summer,
years after her death,
when I peeled the fruit's skin
with my teeth, tasted
part of her flesh.

Lessons from the Flood

In the dark, voices were drowned,
and near dawn Grandma stopped reading,
placed a mark in the family bible
where the book of rain ended. She told us
to take care, that we'd do well
to memorize where the tractors
and horses were washed away, the spot
the neighbor's house fell. Three days later,
in the first shaft of sun, Grandpa unfolded
a Barlow knife, notched a sycamore
where the highest waters reached.
He had us stand, backs to trunk, showed us
how far under the waves we'd have been.
We held our breath, decided it was time
to learn how to swim.   43

The Mennonite's Daughter Goes
Down to the River

and slips the covering from her hair, withdrawing the pins

  that hold the bun, allowing strands to drift down her back

and around her face, pushing her way into water,

  the stream taking the shape of her nose, sunken

eyes, the cleft of her chin, so when she draws back, raises

  her head for the sun to warm, with its pressed flesh

against hers, the imprint of her visage does not vanish

  but travels the watercourse, amazed by what it can see,

the prism of what is above and what is below:

  fish fanning over sunken stones; the contrail of a jet

splitting the sky; the hidden refuse of a refrigerator

  with a turtle asleep on its shelf; the trenched sides

of the channel, evidence of the flood's last licking.

  She is no longer imprisoned, no longer controlled

by a neck anchored to a body. Like the deer she spied

  in the honeysuckle thicket, antlers tangled and fused

in the branches. Velvet rubbed to green, and the green

flowing down the limbs to the base of the skull. Washing

brow tines, dissolving boney sockets, shading irises.

A field of vision the color of sprouting rye

and winter wheat.

First Kiss

She spoke with the voice of an egret, skin swirled
with the smell of rabbit tobacco. He hid in honeysuckle
to watch her catch dragonflies, blue-green matchsticks
with wings glistening like wax paper. Mamaw called them
snake doctors, claimed they'd follow all manner of slithering,
stitch them back together when they were riven by a shovel
or hoe. The boy snared rat snakes, allowed them to slip
around his wrist and elbow, circle his waist. When the girl passed
on the path between fields, or walking to town along the wagon road,
he thought of wind unsettling muslin, the first hint of darkness
on the threshing floor. She bent to his ear in church, croaked
about the feathers of red-winged black birds, how they resembled
the leather covers of a bible, their whistle-song like the secrets
inked on onionskin paper. The morning she took his hand
on the way to the schoolhouse, pulled him under the bent-down
branches of a hedge apple and kissed him, pecking at his lips
like a flicker grubbing a snag, he remembered the preacher
pushing his head backward in the tank of water, hollering
to the congregation that he was saved.

What My Aunt Virginia Says When She Visits

Our village dead walk the crest where ostrich
fern grow as tall as a broom handle, hiding
sagging white breasts, pale withered chests.
Those of us who are closer to death's divide
follow the invisible line of these movements.
A branch swaying where a red tanager takes flight.
The spiraled song of a hermit thrush, like a hand
that pushes against the solid door of a veiled world.
Near the gap in the mountain that swallows the sun,
a woman I know who died in a house-fire
remembers her husband's skin, how after the ashes
settled, she was able to walk right through him.
And a man who recalls the pain of the clot
in his lung but doesn't remember
driving his truck here, although now he grins
as he trails deer or listens to the drumming
of a grouse. Some have gone missing,
but how else would we go on living
except with senses open? The piquant smell
of spicebush broken. The echoed hammering
of a pileated silenced by the shriek of a rabbit
caught in a fence of teeth. Like all scavengers
we taste what is left for us, forgetting
so much bitterness. Since I am gone too,
please remember what you'd like. Selfishly
I've taken with me the sound of my first born,
nursing in the dark hours of morning, steady
breathing as he drifts back to sleep
on the swell of my breast.

Lineage

The boy who will be my mother's father
climbs the mountainside behind the farm,
chestnut trees fencing the ridges, trunks

so large his uncles, arm to arm, can't ring them.
In midsummer the blossoms hang in strands,
like his mother's hair which she lets down

before sleep to brush with an ivory comb
that was a wedding present from her husband's
parents. The spiked hulls drop when the night turns

colder, unlocked like a jewelry box. In October
he harvests all morning, nut's brown skin
sun-glistened, stops at noon to eat a ham sandwich,

smoke and salt seasoning his hands, oiling
the nuts he shovels into a burlap sack.
Every mountain in this part of Virginia is cloaked

in the wealth of board feet and mast, and no one
can imagine it disappearing like a raft in rapids,
lost to blight or the dammed rivers that will flood

this valley. His family's too poor to afford a camera,
but he's seen the well-to-do carry their baskets
up the ridge to pose and picnic beneath these giants.

When the boy is an old man, working a rubber factory,
lungs blackened from cigarettes, eyes watery
with booze and sentiment, he'll sit me on his lap,

point to a picture in a book of a man in a hat
standing on a ladder, wife cradling their child,
a chestnut tree sawn in half.

What Water Wants

The sky clings to rain and won't let go.

      After eight weeks the ground cracks,

and the stream that shows us the way

      through the gap in the mountain

wilts. What little water is left

      wants to comfort speckled trout,

caress caddis larvae attached to the bottomsides

      of rocks. The stumps in the reservoir

peer above waterline, suspicious of the sky

      they haven't seen in years.

My neighbor points at a chimney

      in the middle of the lake, a steeple

a little closer to shore. He tells me

      how his father milked cows, put them out

to pasture before the dam was built,

how the old water that flowed

down the mountain would've never wanted

to drown a valley.

Valley Maker

deep in white clouds,
forever empty, silent.
—HAN SHAN

In darkness the valley floats
along a cloud-river that masks
the one flowing beneath it.

The glacier's tongue that cut
this groove is gone, as is the flood
that left this basin strewn with rubble.

We use a stone-boat to ferry rock
from the field, trying to coax anything
to grow in the coal-ash that drifts
from the fires we set.

Wherever the sickle bar cuts
wheat shines, wet and forgiving,
like our mother's tears
when she tells us how her eyes
have grown dim.

Memory

My long-ago life rises into lone thoughts
and drifts windblown—too much for me.
—TU MU

Honeysuckle greens and spills in the bottom edges
of the woods, buttery petals slicking the light. A bear follows

the fiction of a trail, leaf duff lit and the first violets emerging.
The earliest insect hatches pass over the stream, blue-winged olives

that brook trout devour, betraying themselves with a desperate hunger.
How many new beginnings are we granted? In undisturbed places

Oxalis rings the northern hemisphere, flower's pink stripes flaring
like a small fish's gill plate. Ten autumns ago, hidden

in the field's tall grasses, my son lay his head in my lap,
looked up at the birds flying south and asked how old the sky was.

We'd risen early to listen to migrating thrushes, to see them
take flight from the trees before they vanished.

I told him they followed the moon's slivered path, the same
ancient corridor we use when we leave the earth.

53

Native Species

At work he found himself looking at paintings of deer on the Internet.
Some dead, some dying, others resting in tall grass or beneath green
boughs, the gentle sound of water rolling over stone in the stream
that bordered the picture and flowed out of the frame. Tracking a
doe through briar and multiflora rose, he'd feel the ease of the deer's
movements, the muscle that shaped kinship with the mountain. For
him the trail was precarious, one boot in front of the other as he scaled
steep talus or sunk to his waist in the sloggy alder swamps where
many took refuge: cold soaking skin, changing his own scent. While
laboring with a meat saw, he protested that he loved what he killed,
offering elaborate prayers of thanksgiving for the animal that fed his
family. When winter grew deep, he found the earthen bowls where
they slept, heat of their bodies melting snow, and close by a shed antler,
like a crown removed before sleep. Trimming a hang nail, he began to
suspect something. Plate dark and thick, black as bituminous coal. He
told his wife he'd banged his fingers in a door, but soon his toes divided
as well—three to one side, two to the other, a slant with angular curves
that made wearing shoes impractical. His wife insisted he see a doctor.
Instead he went to the woods where his back bent and lengthened,
neck drawn out, eyes brought to the side, dusky and knowing. Still
she recognized him, clasped his face under the muzzle, scolded him
for procrastinating, while pressing her forehead to his, stroking the
coarse hair along his chest and belly. During rifle season, when the
family heard a shot roll up the valley, they ran to the porch and called
his name, waiting for the comfort of a tail's flash along treeline. His
sons were careful to mark the shape of the ivory patch at the base of his
throat and swore only to hunt squirrel and rabbit. His daughter, who
loved to ride his shoulders, tied yellow yarn from his brow tines in a
cat's cradle. Beneath moonlight, on late summer evenings, he ate the
beets and clover she planted in the garden, stamped his hoof in dark
soil, until a face appeared at the window to look down on velvet antlers,
illuminated like branches in wet snow.

The Turtle

*For the Men and Women Murdered in the Emanuel African
Methodist Episcopal Church, Charleston, South Carolina*

The snapping turtle that crosses the riffles
where I fish is older than I am and descends
from prehistory with lumbering steps.
The shell on its back carries the world
while parting the waters that rush
around us. Nine people were shot
in a church while praying. So many
sacred stories about how turtle
was formed, how out of darkness
stars began to shine, the sun gathering
planets to its breast. A child must be taught
hatred and how to love a gun. This turtle
will bury her eggs in the sand, then retreat
into the river to swim toward home.
In the deepest pools, I hear the voices
of the bereaved singing.

Taxidermy: Cathartes aura

When the vulture fell
from the sky, the boy gathered
the outstretched wings and folded
the body to his breast, feathers
cresting his shoulder, a span
of plumage for riding thermals,
drifting ever higher
above the earth.

The bird's spiraling descent
was unexpected like when
his uncle touched him
in the cellar as he shoveled
coal for winter, telling him
he couldn't have the fried
doughnuts sprinkled
with confectioner's sugar
if he screamed
or told his mother.

Over the next week
the boy slit the dead bird
from neck to tail feathers,
pulled out what had grown inside,
and used cornstarch to dry
the wet residue. He wished to keep
some semblance of the bird
alive before the memory
migrated and was forgotten.

His uncle's white whiskers
stung his cheeks, coffee-breath
at his ear demanding he remove
his pants and later wash
the blood-soaked underwear
at the sink in the garage.

While he worked, tears fell
into the dark space
he'd opened to insert
wires beneath the wings,
around the fragile ribs.
It hurt to sit and burned
when he bore down, excrement
swirled red in the toilet.

In the days that followed
his uncle wanted more,
but the boy begged,
and the man made him take it
in the mouth instead.

He woke with decay in his nostrils
and tried to figure the nature
of the bird's death, but found no bullet
or pebbled buckshot, no evidence
to explain any of this.

He assumed it would go on
until he was older, big enough
to drive a fist into his uncle's throat,
or for that man to keel over,
heart given out while skinning
a raccoon he'd trapped
or turning sod in the garden.

The boy believed the bird
had become the thing
it coveted, having consumed
so much dead flesh, and he stuffed
the cavity with rags and cotton,
sewed the incision and dangled it
with fishing-line over his bed.

Each night before he closed his eyes,
he stared at the pink head, the only
resurrection he believed in now,
and when his mother extinguished
the hall light, he prayed
to the shadow that hung above
to show him how to take flight.

For the First Nine Months We Perceive
the World through the Eyes of Our Mother

Where snow formed
a bridge, water swirls
and bucks with melt
and rain. Upstream

a winterkilled deer
floats, a spike
with eight-inch
antlers, not a single
curve or tine.

Something
cleared its chest
with teeth, ate
most of the meat,
then abandoned
the body. I think

of moving the corpse
onto the bank
but worry about
denying the trout
and crayfish.

With no leaves
the forest lets
the sun drop
aimlessly,

and the river
cleans itself
with water
from smaller
streams.

The Mink

Our eyes locked, and someone threw away the key.
—ANNIE DILLARD

Each morning before school
she runs her father's traps,
a thirty-minute walk
along the creekbed
where darkness surrenders
to the cone of light
from her headlamp.

The mink she's caught
holds still in the snare
as she reaches into the backpack
for her father's .22 pistol,
only to be drawn
if the pelt is worth killing for.

Danger, her grandfather says,
is peering into the eyes of the animal
you must shoot. Simply place
the muzzle at the back of the skull
and squeeze the trigger.

She's felt the recoil, like the shake
of muscle when she plays
with the black snake that lives
under the porch. But before
she can click the safety,
the mink's eyes pull her in,
until she stares out from a skull
that's not her own.

She's surprised not to feel fear.
Nor does she harbor hope.
Simple resignation
to wait for the bars
grasping her leg
to open. That strange,
toothless mouth
yawning in boredom.

She remembers what the mink
remembers. Comfort of water.
Song rubbing against stone.
If freedom finds her again,
she'll sing a hymn of thanks
to the moving current
she's saved
within her chest.

When she was a girl she swam
in the quarry, diving from a ledge
into the sky's reflection.
That's what it's like inside this skull:
legs kicking deeper into a rock-cut pit.

And she wonders what the mink
must think of its new body.
The uprightness. The loss of fluidity.
But also the weight of that gun.
The decision whether to let her go,
or to bring this body back
for her father to skin
and sell at market.

A Senior Citizen at the Good Shepherd and Water of Life Assisted Living Center Asks Her Son for a Sky Burial

She reads about it in a *National Geographic* that she takes home in
her purse from the doctor's office. With glasses perched atop her
head like a tufted titmouse, she presses her face to the pages, nearly
touching the glossy veneer with her nose, trying to peek under the
fingernails that curve at the end of the dead hand and the Buddhist
monk who ceremonially dismembers the body with an ax. She gasps
at the wingspan of the vulture that pecks at fingers and forearm, trying
to judge if it can lift the appendage and still get off the ground. The
next morning over coffee she shows her son the magazine, tells him
that's what she wants: to be eaten and dispersed by birds, last will and
testament of her skin. She's no Buddhist, having played the organ and
taught Sunday School in the Tipton United Methodist Church, but she
still isn't exactly sure what happens to the soul when the body fails. She
likes to believe it migrates into the lives of other creatures, becomes
a fox or frog, an ant in a colony serving a queen, a red salamander
entering a pond before it freezes. Her best friend Sally thinks it floats up
towards Christ, a little lower than the stratosphere, where its light sifts
through the clouds, that yellowy cast they saw on the senior bus tour to
Cape Cod when they walked the beach without shoes. To her, it makes
more sense to be eaten in the treetops, meat rent by beaks and flown
over the mountains where her dead husband hunted. Who wants to be
roasted in an oven, or, worse yet, put in a box to molder? Her son tries
to explain that if she goes missing, folks will start looking. She tells him
to say she's gone to visit relatives in West Virginia. He'll need a sturdy
rope to throw over a tall bough, a sailor's knot around her ankles. The
branch will serve as a cantilever to haul her towards the sky. She says it's
fine to leave her in one piece. She wouldn't insist that he use an ax like
the monk. She asks him to visit in January, to check on her bones, the
last strands of tendon that will bind her skeleton like a wind chime.

63

Dead Letter to James Wright

It's been a long time
in the ditch. Snowmelt
and most of May
the river muddy.
By July jewelweed
blossoms, then wild
carrot in August
and ironweed
in September.
There are so many
flowers I can't name.
Privet multiplies, garlic
mustard colonizes
the understory. You said
you'd wasted your life.
I'm still not sure
what species I am.

III.

Seep

It pleases me, loving rivers.
Loving them all the way back
to their source.
—RAYMOND CARVER

It was the fish that kept us climbing.
April already and last fall's spawning
still striped their sides. With snowmelt
the stream washed white, and two miles up

we knew we sought the beginning.
Like the trout we caught, we navigated
against the current, searching for sky
through thinning trees. Near the ridge,

the land flattened, the water slowed.
We followed the sound to a cleft
where a spring comes out of the ground,
as it has for ten thousand years.

We dipped our hands, tasted the oldest
cold in our mouths: source of iron and stone,
the moon and the tides it controls,
the dimming blood we share.

Generosity

The sun hits the ice-coated snow at 186,282 miles per second,
then slides across the greased surface of the earth.

I woke our sons this morning with the smell of bacon
spitting in an iron skillet.

An hour earlier, the smell of your sex stirred me,
and we held each other in dim light

as a garbage truck rumbled through the neighborhood.
I crack eggs in the brown the bacon bequeaths,

whisk them until the yellow and white congeal.
This time of year I have to squint to make out the heads

of laurel leaves as they strain their necks
to stay above snowline. With so much radiance

it's hard to hide my love for the pleasures of the earth.
When I was ten, a maple tree, split at its crotch by lightning,

wept sap, freezing and thawing in an amber slick.
Night turned over in an unmade bed, and I licked

the sweet until my tongue was raw. What compares
to a cheek on the breast, a hand gently cradling

a lover's bottom? Near the middle of the river
frazil ice swirls and bucks, kicking water into the air

where it freezes. You love dark chocolate and sea salt,
anything that melts with the body's temperature.

I love building a fire in the snow, watching the russet
soil appear beneath the kettle as it begins to boil.

The Rain that Holds Light in the Trees

Two months ago ice stacked up along the river's banks, thin
panes flipped by the wind. Some of the glass still fractures,
glistening brighter in its brokenness.

My grandmother told me that deer store their souls in antlers
and in winter shed them, visible spirits returning to the bone
beneath the forehead. On the coldest days, shorn reeds whistle

a music composed from wind and hollow stubs, an improvised
panpipe showering the silence. Evolution folded our brains
back and forth like taffy, skulls expanding, neck muscles growing

to support the weight of thought. Our mothers' pelvises
accommodated the soul's stretching as well, loosening joints
and soft tissue, squeezing us into a world we've dissected

and categorized, yet still know so little about. In Australia
biologists observe black kites and brown falcons descending
along the periphery of wildfires: wing-beat and talon-grasp,

a burning branch transported to start new fires. Our desire
to know more, to carry more of what we know with us,
causes us to forget that time is a swirl of stars, a constellation

of galaxies, a dream we can't remember when we wake.
The hippocampus in squirrel allows them to remember
where they've cached acorns and hickory nuts, the same

spatial cognition that helps me write about the bend
where Loup Run turns west along a talus field, sun low,
piercing poles of moosewood and black birch. In a note

I found in an old journal, I place myself behind my father:
a boy trying to walk in footprints spaced too far apart.
My father, who was younger than I am today, was afraid

I might step on a copperhead as we picked blackberries
for the batter my mother poured into a greasy skillet, flour
butter-crisped like gold leaf. Along the banks where the last

of the river water is frozen, holding out against its own passing
and the water's rising, our tracks are washing away. Ravens
and crows fall to the field just beyond tree line, eating remnants

of last year's corn, then fly up to the tallest branches
where clouds gather, bringing with them the rain
that holds light in the trees.

Gnosis

In a blue river made of snowmelt
that forms this valley of aspen and alder,

I fish with my sons until summer's light fades
in the recesses of a canyon.

While hunting alone I entered a small cave
to take shelter from a passing squall

and found the bones of a bear cub
curled in a circle of trust.

Someday when the white fields disappear
and only rain falls from the heavens,

this river will vanish too.
The trout we catch have throats that shine

with a bright red mark, suggesting the role
blood plays in betrayal.

A woman who is long dead told me
that when a river passes away, it holds

the memory of itself in the silt left behind.
When our species is extinct,

what animal will carry the memory
of our lives?

Waiting to Hear If a Friend's Wife Has Cancer

All morning outside my window, in the purple
flowers of the redbud, bumblebees, fat
on what the world feeds them, glide
between turning branches. All morning
the tree's blossoms caress the backs
of these bees in what seems a delicate
balance between love and need. All morning
the wind scatters the petals into the air
and onto the grasses. All morning finches
and sparrows share this tree's branches,
never colliding with the bees. All morning
the sun lavishes the air with praise for the places
where the flowers fell away and where now
the smallest leaves unfurl. All morning
I imagine the drive to Pittsburgh, the small
sterile room, the fluorescent light tracing
the almost imperceptible hairs
along the oncologist's lips
as she begins to speak.

For Chris and Brian Black

Notes on the Anniversary of the Death of Galway Kinnell

Sunlight glints on spider threads
spanning a chasm of branches.

*

Where my neighbor shot a deer
opening day of hunting season
a smear of blood, bits of fur
we'll find after winter recedes
and the arbutus blooms.

*

We stick to the earth,
whether something in us
departs or not.

*

Where you walked to the pond, along
the failing wall at the edge of the woods,
the shape of your coming and going
has yet to disappear.

*

Today, in the crown of a hemlock, a porcupine
eats a circle of bark, sap beginning to run
from the wound, sticky like honey, smelling
like overturned earth after a hard rain.

*

Kotodama is the Japanese belief
that mystical powers
dwell in words.

*

For the past week, outside my window,
a crow has been repeating your name.

After Twenty-Seven Years of Marriage

I imagine your soul is the texture of cantaloupe
as you bend over the tub to wash your hair.

100 million years is a long time to migrate, but
the warblers flying through the black gum trees

outside our window navigate the same space
as their ancestors. The cat, descended from Egypt,

sleeps in the crook of your legs
with the expectation that we will rub her

under the chin and down the bridge of her nose.
In the morning a storm sacrifices more than six

inches of rain, and now a cow bobs down the river,
rolling from side to side. You collected toy horses

as a child because your father was poor and drank away
the hay, the stall doors, the paddock fencing.

After correcting me about how your soul feels,
you feed me pink slices of watermelon.

I drown happily in the sweetness
of your company.

Dead Letter to Richard Hugo

An abandoned pickup
rusts near a trailer
whose roof has caved in.

Along the valley floor
wood smoke loiters
and won't move on.

My friend's wife says
he needs to get a job
so he heads to the reservoir
and catches three trout.

There's a *For-Sale* sign
in front of the church. High up
still some stained glass, but
all the pews in the sanctuary
remain empty.

Dirt roads map everything
in squares before dead-ending
at the base of mountains.

The TV antenna
that peaks our roof
is a homily to the lack
of our ambition.

Although it's late
in the year, I dream
of a yellow-rumped warbler
singing outside the window.

When I rise to look,
wind whistles
through a small bird's
skeleton.

With Nothing Between Us and the End of the World

After a line by Shann Ray

Another hot, dry summer. Cutthroat swim from the main river into the north fork, waiting for October and November: gray days with the possibility for rain, then snow. I'm here alone, our sons having drifted into lives of their own. On the phone you tell me the butternut squash have ripened, the final tomatoes green. A shadow swirls from between rocks as a trout rises to a fly outlined by the sun. Even a few days separation hurts. The absence of your silhouette when you wake in the night, out of habit walking down the hall to look into the boys' room. Water collides, wears away stone, fashioning a new path. This close to such churning I wouldn't hear a bear until it was so near there'd be little to do except pray. We're always at the mercy of the world. I cradle the cutthroat I've drawn from the creek, point its head upstream, allowing cold water to flow through its gills. The fish swivels out of my hands, across the current, like you do after we make love.

Self-Portrait with My Dead

What should I say when my dead visit,

       sometimes as an elk tramping raspberry

canes; other times as a white-footed mouse

       eating the small red fruit

of the barberry from which our neighbor

       makes jelly? Yesterday, while working

in the garden, I saw a kestrel on the day's

       warming breath. Last night,

before sleep, an owl called

       through the yellowing tamaracks.

Inside a dream I woke to a hummingbird

       beating its wings

against the roof of my mouth

       and laughed as my grandmother flew

from between my lips. And now,

       as I wake a second time, this curiosity:

a ruby iridescence busies itself, fluttering

on my tongue, sweet and insistent,

asking me to say the names of the dead

again and again.

Logjam on Lookout Creek

The country in ruins, rivers and mountains
continue.
—TU FU

I sit on 1500 years snagged
       by its collective weight, by the downward pull
of this valley, and the simple force of water
       when it meets snowmelt and rain.
How long these logs will stay is anyone's guess.
       Stoneflies have hatched in this place of rest,
time-tempered, bent and slowed by the sound
       of creek bumping against pushed up gravel:
a change of structure bending,
       the plummeting of water slackened, guided
and gilded by slivers of light etched
       with hemlock needles and fir boughs,
with a shadow-show of alder cones reformed
       into a pool of the coldest clarity.
If you pick up part of this river,
       turn over a stone, you'll find it's connected
to everything else—pupa caddis and cutthroat,
       sculpin and rough-skinned newt. The very trees
whose crowns rise higher than I can see. Some
       will come crashing in hundred-year floods;
others—after feeding pileateds and beetles—
       will lie down to fashion failed dams
that momentarily change the course, current
       diverted, carrying part of these mountains
on toward the cities of our ruins.

Appalachian Nocturne: Ursa Major

By the second week of November, the apples we haven't scavenged
populate the ground. The night sky looks down on an old sow bear,

likely in her last year, as she wanders between trees searching
for rotting windfalls. She gorges on McIntosh, winesap, the now-

sweetened bitterness of northern spy, preparing for the lean
months ahead. Around midnight we hear her stumble against

the wooden locker where trash is stored. With light from the moon
like ash, we see a silhouette, our headlamps sending out small circles

to save us. The first people told a story of hunters who pursued
a bear, blood spattering leaves after a spear pierced its side.

As the year wanes the last animal colors glow, and the skeleton
of that myth staggers across the sky on all fours. Some nights we walk

to the dam to listen to trapped water escape down the retention wall.
Below the dam speckled trout try to swim upstream to spawn.

I pray my sons will live to see the stones undone. I'll miss the sow
if she doesn't wake in spring. A barred owl calls out a prophecy,

notes scaling the constellation we've named. Where darkness gathers,
stars fall. Strings of light tying heaven to earth.

Returning to Earth

At the bottom of an abandoned well
dug more than a century ago
the moon rises from the center
of the earth, a crust of ice
forming around its edges.

The stand of larch outside
our bedroom window
sways, golden needles
stirring the air
underneath its boughs.

I open the window to hear
the river sailing away, riding
the stone boat of the basin
carved by spring floods.

Beyond the faint light
of a candle, your voice asks
if we might touch and remember
how our children were made,
how the bodies of our parents
were returned to earth.

I want our children's hands
to hold the river, to watch it spill
through their fingers, back to a source
older than our names
for God.

Beneath a waxing moon
we've witnessed animals
dragging their dead into the light.
Tonight we imagine some
suckling their young
who are born blind
in these coldest months.

Soon the river will freeze,
and come morning we'll break
the ice in the well
so we may drink.

In dark's shelter I place the words
of a prayer upon your tongue.
You are gracious, saying
the prayer back
into my waiting mouth.

Thankful for Now

Walking the river back home at the end
of May, locust in bloom, an oriole flitting
through dusky crowns, and the early night sky
going peach, day's late glow the color of that fruit's
flesh, dribbling down over everything, christening
my sons, the two of them walking before me
after a day of fishing, one of them placing a hand
on the other's shoulder, pointing toward a planet
that's just appeared, or the swift movement
of that yellow and black bird disappearing
into the growing dark, and now the light, pink
as a crabapple's flower, and my legs tired
from wading the higher water, and the rocks
that keep turning over, nearly spilling me
into the river, but still thankful for now
when I have enough strength to stay
a few yards behind them, loving this time
of day that shows me the breadth
of their backs, their lean, strong legs
striding, how we all go on in this cold water,
heading home to the sound of the last few
trout splashing, as mayflies float
through the shadowed riffles.

Coltrane Eclogue

You can play a shoestring if you're sincere.
—JOHN COLTRANE

Where the beak of a pileated opened a row
of holes down the length of a snag
wind blows across each notch,
angles of breathing, like Saint Coltrane
unfastening pearl and brass, exhalation
rushing through the neck of a saxophone,
bending into the sound that envelops
anyone with ears to hear. I've started to chant
a love supreme, although I'm alone,
more than four miles into the crease,
trying to pick up the rhythm, how each
lungful glides through hemlock needles,
kestrel slipping out onto the updraft,
with one wing-beat shifting the air
ever so slightly. And yet another woodpecker
drilling the side of a dying tree, a northern
flicker that stays just out of sight, laying down
a percussive line. I feel foolish for saying this,
but it's like being reborn, a syncopation
that can call down rain, make the bud of a shadbush
unfurl, unwrap the slow, honest tongues
of beaver, and stamp a moose's enormous
hind-quarter like a bass, all the others silenced,
fingers of that long-dead saint scaling gut-strings,
before a Blackburnian warbler joins in with its thin,
plaintive notes, and a goddamned bluebird,
which should seem trivial but is not, breast puffed,
raising its head toward a God that surrounds us,
who opens our stupid mouths and commands us
to play whatever instrument we've got.

And If There Is a Day of Resurrection

then on that day may the water in the creek shimmer

green, a music never heard take shape in a hatch

of caddis and coffin flies, the air bluing as the sun's light

dries insect wings, and the bear skull on the ridge,

the circle of porcupine quills, the mink's eye sockets

and the coyote's hinged jaw still clutched around the rabbit's femur,

may all the bones of the living and the dead rise

with skeletal praise, this ancient world being remade

in their image.

ACKNOWLEDGMENTS

My thanks to the editors of the following journals or publications in which these poems first appeared, sometimes in different form.

About Place Journal: "Generosity" and "Geomorphology"
Alaska Quarterly Review: "Goat's Milk"
Anglers Journal: "Thankful for Now"
The Antigonish Review: "A Senior Citizen at the Good Shepherd and Water of Life Assisted Living Center Asks Her Son for a Sky Burial"
Appalachia: "Hexagonal," "Perception," and "What Water Wants"
Appalachian Heritage: "The Mink"
Artful Dodge: "The Mennonite's Daughter Goes Down to the River"
Arts & Letters: "What My Aunt Virginia Says When She Visits"
Atlanta Review: "With Nothing Between Us and the End of the World"
Barrow Street: "Almanac of Faithful Negotiations"
Blueline: "Seep"
Chautauqua: "Hibernation"
Chariton Review: "After Twenty-Seven Years of Marriage."
Cold Mountain Review: "How Our Names Turn into Light"
The Gettysburg Review: "Decadence" and "Passerine"
Harmony: "Waiting to Hear If a Friend's Wife Has Cancer"
Hiram Poetry Review: "Hard Winter"
The Hollins Critic: "Talus Slope"
The Hopper: "Finding a Skull"
Image: "First Kiss" and "First Thoughts about God after Spying a Speckled Trout Eat a Green Drake"
ISLE: "Appalachian Nocturne: *Ursa Major*"
The Louisville Review: "The Turtle"
The Missouri Review: "Taxidermy: *Cathartes aura*"

Natural Bridge: "In the Seventh Month My Mother Worries" and
  "Lessons from the Flood"
North American Review: "The Rain that Holds Light in the Trees"
Orion: "And If There Is a Day of Resurrection"
Paterson Literary Review: "Geodes"
Permafrost: "The Woman Who Cuts My Hair"
Pinyon: "17-Year Locust" and "Denomination"
Poet Lore: "Lost Country of Light"
Poetry East: "My Mother's Cooking"
Poetry Northwest: "Coltrane Eclogue"
Rattle: "Cracks"
Ruminate: "Returning to Earth"
Sycamore Review: "Green Beans"
Tar River Poetry: "Dead Letter to James Wright"
Terrain.org: "Logjam on Lookout Creek"

All translations of the quoted lines from the poetry of Han Shan, Mei Yao-Ch'en, Tu Fu, Tu Mu, and Yang Wan-Li are by David Hinton.

Thanks to the following people for their continued encouragement as I make my poems: Jan Beatty, Lori Bechtel-Wherry, Brian Black, Craig Blietz, Marcia and Bruce Bonta, Dave Bonta, Taylor Brorby, Lauren Camp, Cameron Conaway, James Crews, Jim Daniels, Geffrey Davis, Joyce Davis, Nathan Davis, Shelly Davis, Alison Hawthorne Deming, Chris Dombrowski, David James Duncan, Stephen Dunn, Tom Montgomery Fate, Don Flenar, Don and Punky Fox, Ross Gay, Dan Gerber, Andy Gottlieb, Virginia Kasamis, Helen Kiklevich, Don and Melinda Lanham, Mary Linton, Julie Loehr, Adrian Matejka, Michael McDermott, Sarah McDonald, Carolyn Mahan, Dinty Moore, Erin Murphy, Aimee Nezhukumatathil, Mary Rose O'Reilley, Sean Prentiss, Derek Sheffield, Julie Reaume, Jack Ridl, Pattiann Rogers, Annette Tanner, Patricia Jabbeh Wesley, Joe Wilkins, and Ken Womack.

A special thanks to five wonderful writers who read this book in various stages and helped to make it better: Noah Davis, K. A. Hays, Lee Peterson, Steve Sherrill, and Dave Shumate.

I would also like to thank the H. J. Andrews Experimental Forest in Oregon for a writer's residency and the Black Earth Institute for a three-year fellowship that helped with the writing of this book.

Many of these poems were finished with the assistance of generous grants from Pennsylvania State University, including a sabbatical and a fellowship in the Institute for the Arts & Humanities.

Todd Davis is the author of six full-length collections of poetry—*Native Species, Winterkill, In the Kingdom of the Ditch, The Least of These, Some Heaven*, and *Ripe*—as well as of a limited-edition chapbook, *Household of Water, Moon, and Snow*. He edited the nonfiction collection, *Fast Break to Line Break: Poets on the Art of Basketball*, and co-edited the anthology *Making Poems*. His writing has won the Foreword INDIES Book of the Year Bronze and Silver Awards, the Gwendolyn Brooks Poetry Prize, the Chautauqua Editors Prize, and has been nominated several times for the Pushcart Prize. His poems appear in such noted journals and magazines as *Alaska Quarterly Review, American Poetry Review, Barrow Street, Gettysburg Review, Iowa Review, Missouri Review, North American Review, Orion, Poetry Northwest, Sycamore Review, West Branch*, and *Poetry Daily*. He teaches environmental studies, creative writing, and American literature at Pennsylvania State University's Altoona College.